SPOT THE DIFFERENCES

Art Masterpiece Mysteries

DOVER PUBLICATIONS, INC.
Mineola, New York

Series Concept and Project Editor: Diane Teitel Rubins
Design Concept: Alan Weller
Designer: Juliana Trotta
Senior Editor: Susan L. Rattiner

Copyright

Bibliographical Note

Spot the Differences: Art Masterpiece Mysteries, Book 3 is a new work, first published by Dover Publications, Inc., in 2012.

International Standard Book Number
ISBN-13: 978-0-486-48085-5
ISBN-10: 0-486-48085-2

Manufactured in the United States by Courier Corporation
48085201
www.doverpublications.com

How well do you truly know the great masterpieces of fine art?

In this book of 25 famous paintings, you will find anywhere from 9 to 13 changes that were made to the originals—from some very obvious differences all the way down to the tiniest little detail. The original painting and the one in which we have made changes are side by side, so you must inspect them both ever so carefully! Just remember: the original work of art always appears on the *left* side! Use your keen observational skills to compare the two pages, and see if you can detect all the differences that appear on the right side of the page. As you discover the differences, remember to keep score by checking the boxes provided on each puzzle page.

Once you have finished strolling through this outstanding gallery of images, you may go to page 54 to check your answers to the puzzles. Try not to peek, though, until you have tried your best to find all the changes! As you go along through the book, you'll learn exciting facts about each painting and its artist. This book is a wonderful and fun introduction to some of the world's greatest works of art.

Giuseppe Arcimboldo
Summer (1573)

Arcimboldo began his career as a designer of stained glass windows depicting scenes from the lives of the saints.

Arcimboldo was known for his creativity and playful sense of humor. He would cleverly arrange everyday objects to form human faces.

This picture belongs to his Four Seasons series, and features different kinds of summer fruits and vegetables.

On the collar of the figure, he has artfully included his name followed by the letter "F," which stands for the Latin word, *fecit*, meaning "he did it." It is a word often inscribed after the name of an artist or sculptor.

Royalty greatly admired Arcimboldo. In 1562 he became the court portraitist to Maximilian II and later to Rudolf II, Maximilian's son.

In addition to his work as a portraitist, Arcimboldo was also a court decorator, costume designer, and "event planner," overseeing all of the royal festivities.

Keep Score:
9 Changes

☐ ☐ ☐ ☐ ☐
☐ ☐ ☐ ☐

Pieter Bruegel the Elder
Children's Games (1560)

Bruegel provided a very detailed view of children's play in medieval Europe. Although many of the activities seen here might be familiar today, there are a few that do not exist anymore.

There's lots of lively activity in this 16th-century painting and, the longer you look at it, the more there is to see. There are young children everywhere in this painting—some are pretending to be horses, doing acrobatics, and playing tug of war and leapfrog, while others are playing with hoops and spinning tops.

This painting includes nearly 200 children playing almost 80 different games and outdoor activities!

Bruegel had two sons, Pieter the Younger and Jan. When both boys grew up to be artists, their father became known as Pieter Bruegel the Elder, to distinguish his paintings from those of his sons.

The artist is known by the nickname "Peasant Bruegel" since he often shows peasants in their everyday lives within his paintings.

Keep Score: **13 Changes** ☐ ☐ ☐ ☐ ☐ ☐ ☐ ☐ ☐ ☐ ☐ ☐ ☐

Mary Cassatt
Tea (1879-80)

The silver tea set that Cassatt included in this painting was part of a family set made in Philadelphia about 1813. These pieces are now in the collection of the Museum of Fine Arts in Boston.

Mary Cassatt was one of only three women—and the only American—ever to join the French Impressionists, a small group of independent French artists.

Although born in America, Mary spent most of her adult life in Paris.

Although she never had any children of her own, Cassatt is perhaps best known for her paintings of mothers and children and the love they share.

The United States Postal Service issued two commemorative stamps in honor of Mary Cassatt. The first, appearing in 1966, was a five-cent stamp picturing *The Boating Party*. The second, issued in 1988, was a twenty-three-cent stamp of her portrait.

Keep Score: **10 Changes** ☒ ☒ ☒ ☒ ☒ ☒ ☒ ☐ ☐ ☐

Paul Cézanne
The Cardplayers (1890-92)

Cézanne believed that everything in the world was made up of a sphere, a cone, a cylinder, or a cube. He began many of his works using these basic shapes.

Cézanne painted five different versions of this scene, which depicts a group of peasants playing cards. In all of the versions, he emphasizes the serious expressions of the players, each one concentrating intensely on the game.

Cézanne is often described as "the Father of Modern Art."

One of Cézanne's *Cardplayers* paintings recently sold at auction to the country of Qatar for an amazing $250 million!

Keep Score: 9 Changes ☐ ☐ ☐ ☐ ☐ ☐ ☐ ☐ ☐

William Merritt Chase
A Friendly Call (1895)

The painter's wife, Alice Gerson Chase, sits on the right, and greets a guest, who has not yet removed her gloves, hat, or put down her parasol. Due to the strict social etiquette of the 1890s, a guest had to wait until the hostess asked before she was allowed to do so.

Indiana-born Chase is best known for his portraits, landscapes, and still lifes. In his twenties, Chase was so excited to study art abroad that he claimed, "I'd rather go to Europe than go to heaven!"

This painting takes place in the artist's studio at his summer home in Long Island, New York. Artistic influences from the Orient are evident in the bamboo chair and silk wall hangings in the room.

An American Impressionist, Chase used a large mirror in this picture to reflect a sunny hallway with a small stairway leading to his studio.

While at the Royal Academy in Munich, Chase painted with a dark and somber palette. However, a tour in Venice turned his interest toward the impressionistic effects of light, and his landscapes soon reflected this influence.

Chase taught at a variety of art academies for nearly forty years and touched the lives of many future artists such as Edward Hopper and Charles Sheeler.

Keep Score: **11 Changes** ☐ ☐ ☐ ☐ ☐ ☐ ☐ ☐ ☐ ☐ ☐

Jacques-Louis David

The Emperor Napoleon in His Study at the Tuileries (1812)

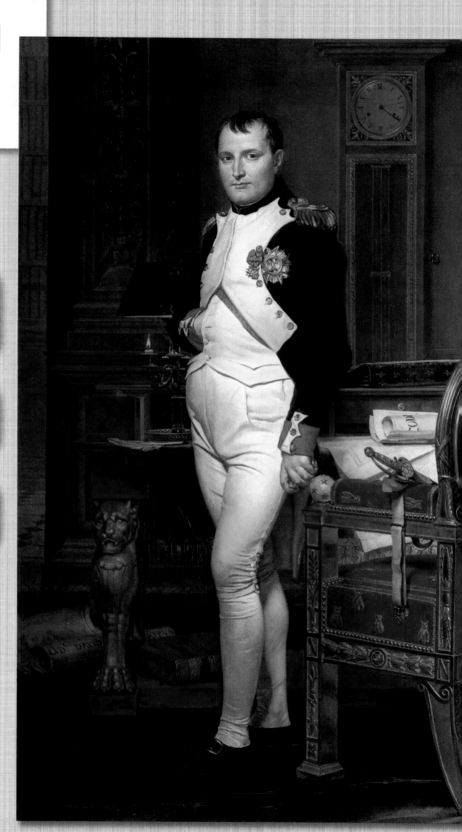

A history painter in the Neoclassical style, David had a large number of art students, making him the strongest influence on French art in the early nineteenth century.

David was Napoleon's official artist, and was trusted to create a painting that showed his employer in a most flattering way.

Art enthusiasts appreciate the portraits by David since they reveal a depth of fascinating information about their sitters.

Born to a rich Parisian family, David was sent to live with his architect uncles after his father was killed in a duel. Though his family wanted him to be an architect, David aspired to be a painter instead, and attended the Royal Academy in France.

In addition to his historical paintings, David completed a number of privately commissioned portraits.

Keep Score:

13 Changes

☐ ☐ ☐ ☐ ☐
☐ ☐ ☐ ☐ ☐
☐ ☐ ☐

Edgar Degas
Portrait of Edmond Duranty (1879)

The subject of this work, Edmond Duranty, was a wealthy writer and art critic who founded a short-lived magazine. He was also an enthusiastic fan of Impressionism and counted many artists as his friends.

Degas is known as the "Painter of Dancers." His unique scenes of ballerinas have become world famous.

In 1873, Degas was among the founding members of the Impressionist group that also included Pissarro, Monet, and Renoir.

Unlike the other Impressionists, Degas preferred workshop painting and never shared their love for the countryside and painting in open-air settings.

Degas's paintings are filled with new and unique viewpoints that are typical of his work. He often used unusual angles and perspectives to capture brief moments in time.

Thomas Eakins
Max Schmitt in a Single Scull (1871)

Eakins's boyhood friend Max Schmitt turns toward the viewer, and just behind him to the right, is the artist himself pulling the oars of his own boat.

The calm, peaceful setting in this painting takes place on the Schuylkill River in Philadelphia, Pennsylvania.

His memorable scenes of rowing, sailing, and boxing are well known for their vibrant realism and compelling drama.

An amateur rower, Eakins created a series of two dozen paintings that depicted sculling, a rowing sport in which the rower, with one oar in each hand, races backwards toward the finish line. This is the first in his series, celebrating Max Schmitt's victory in the October 1870 race.

Eakins lived in the early days of photography, and he used this new medium to help visualize his paintings.

Keep Score: 10 Changes ☐ ☐ ☐ ☐ ☐ ☐ ☐ ☐ ☐ ☐

Paul Gauguin
When Will You Marry?
(1892)

A restless man, Gauguin traveled and worked in the French regions of Brittany and Provence as well as the South and Central Americas. In 1891, he moved to the French colony of Tahiti in search of an exotic life in "paradise." He spent all but two of the remaining years of his life in the South Seas.

While living in Tahiti, Gauguin painted this picture, as well as other works that depicted the exotic life there. This period formed his now-famous primitive style, which included native figures and landscapes with strong outlines.

Gauguin had a successful career as a stockbroker when he took up painting as a hobby.

His book, *Noa Noa*, described his personal experiences in Tahiti and included some of his sketches and woodcut illustrations. The work was a narrative of his artistic perceptions of his time spent in the South Seas.

Original Gauguin paintings are rarely found for sale. If they are, the asking price could be close to $40 million.

Keep Score:
11 Changes

☐ ☐ ☐ ☐ ☐
☐ ☐ ☐ ☐ ☐
☐

Vincent van Gogh
Starry Night (1889)

Van Gogh created *Starry Night* while staying in an asylum in Saint-Rémy-de-Provence, France. He painted it from memory and not outdoors, as was his usual preference.

Van Gogh sold only one painting in his lifetime—*Red Vineyard at Arles* (now in the Pushkin Museum, Moscow).

In the front of this painting, on the left, is a flamelike cypress tree that bisects a quiet village. Swirling waves of energy seem to burst from the canvas.

Starry Night has become one of the most well-known images in modern culture and has been the subject of poetry, fiction, and even a popular song by Don McLean.

Van Gogh was fascinated with night and wrote to his brother Theo: "It often seems to me that the night is much more alive and richly colored than the day . . . The problem of painting night scenes and effects on the spot and actually by night interests me enormously."

Keep Score: 9 Changes ☐ ☐ ☐ ☐ ☐ ☐ ☐ ☐ ☐

William Harnett
Music and Literature (1878)

Harnett was a master at *trompe-l'oeil* painting—which literally means "to deceive the eye" in French. It refers to an art technique that creates a three-dimensional illusion. In this painting, the objects look so realistic that it feels as if you can just reach out and lift an item off the table.

Harnett was an expert at showing different textures—the music pages stained with age, the shiny flute, the well-worn leather books, and the reflection of light on the candlestick.

Harnett's technical brilliance and reliance on popular subject matter made him the most imitated American still-life painter of his generation.

On the desk is Miguel Cervantes's novel *Don Quixote* (1605) and Giuseppe Verdi's opera *La Traviata* (which was first performed in 1853). The age-worn books and torn music pages signify the obvious passage of time.

Beginning his career as an engraver, Harnett studied at the Pennsylvania Academy and in New York City.

William Hogarth
The Graham Children (1742)

The portrait includes (from left to right): two-year-old Thomas in a gold-leaf go-cart, nine-year-old Henrietta, five-year-old Anna Maria, and seven-year-old Richard, who is playing a mechanical organ.

Sadly, when this picture was completed, the youngest child had died. A number of symbols throughout the painting hint at his tragic death. The flowers at the toddler's feet are a symbol of how quickly life can fade and the dove on his go-cart is a symbol of his young soul flying to heaven.

In the 1730s, Hogarth painted life-sized portraits of the wealthy, and is today considered to be one of the most successful English artists.

The son of a schoolmaster and writer, Hogarth was born in London and apprenticed to a goldsmith. He began to produce his own engraved designs in 1710, and soon became interested in oil painting.

Keep Score: 12 Changes ❑ ❑ ❑ ❑ ❑ ❑ ❑ ❑ ❑ ❑ ❑ ❑

Jean-Auguste-Dominique Ingres
Madame Moitessier (1856)

Influenced by Renaissance art, this portrait depicts the wife of a wealthy banker. The pose is derived from an ancient Roman fresco of a goddess.

Ingres believed that portraiture was not as impressive an art form as history painting and, when he was first commissioned to do this portrait in 1844, he declined. However, after he met his subject, he was struck by her beauty and agreed to paint her portrait.

A pupil of Jacques-Louis David, Ingres studied at the Ècole des Beaux-Arts in Paris. He also won a scholarship to Rome in the early 1800s.

This picture was left unfinished for a period of seven years. In 1851, Ingres painted a standing portrait of Madame Moitessier before returning to the seated portrait that he finally completed in 1856.

Ingres was also a skilled violinist and could have easily pursued a successful career as a musician.

A master of portraiture, Ingres also painted smaller works that illustrated literary texts and scenes from French history.

Keep Score:

9 Changes

☐ ☐ ☐ ☐ ☐

☐ ☐ ☐ ☐

Édouard Manet
The Railroad (1873)

The door and windows in the upper left corner of this painting are those of Manet's studio on the rue de Saint-Pétersbourg.

In this painting, a little girl (likely the daughter of Manet's friend) watches the railroad yards near the artist's studio at the Gare Saint-Lazare station. Her nanny cradles a sleeping puppy in her lap, oblivious to the girl's fascination with the steam engines.

Victorine Meurent, the woman in this picture, was one of Manet's favorite professional models and she posed for several of his paintings, including the famous *Olympia*, which was completed ten years before this one.

Manet painted scenes and people from everyday life as close as possible to the way they actually looked. Because of this approach, he is often described as a realist.

Although Manet was inspired by the Impressionist painters, he never exhibited with them.

Keep Score: 10 Changes ☐ ☐ ☐ ☐ ☐ ☐ ☐ ☐ ☐ ☐

Claude Monet
Terrace at Sainte-Adresse (1867)

The works that Monet created while in Sainte-Adresse during the second half of the 1860s reflect a slight shift in his representation of the sea. This picture has a carefree atmosphere compared to the wild seascapes of his previous years.

Monet spent the summer of 1867 at the resort town of Sainte-Adresse on the English Channel, where he painted this picture. Monet's father is seated in front next to his niece. Monet's cousin and her father stand together at the garden fence.

The print that may have inspired this picture—by the Japanese artist Hokusai—remains at Monet's house at Giverny.

Monet's famous series of haystacks and water lilies are examples of his fascination with the effects of sunlight, time, and weather on his subjects.

Keep Score: 12 Changes ☐ ☐ ☐ ☐ ☐ ☐ ☐ ☐ ☐ ☐ ☐ ☐

Camille Pissarro
Chestnut Trees at Louveciennes (c. 1872)

The sketchy marks in the space between the back of the house and the smaller building on the right suggest windows and the framework of another house and that perhaps Pissarro had intended to do additional work on this painting.

One of the founders of Impressionism, Pissarro studied art in Paris. As the oldest member of a group of fifteen aspiring Impressionist artists, Pissarro was considered a "father figure" to them and later to the major Post-Impressionists, including van Gogh, Cézanne, Gauguin, and Seurat.

In this painting, a parent and child are bundled up against the cold, and are embraced by the arched branches of the chestnut trees above them. Although their faces are not clearly detailed, the woman may be Pissarro's wife, Julie, and their six-year-old daughter Minette.

Pissarro was the only artist to show his work at all eight of the Paris Impressionist exhibitions from 1874 to 1886.

Keep Score: 9 Changes ☐ ☐ ☐ ☐ ☐ ☐ ☐ ☐ ☐

Maurice Prendergast
Central Park (1914-15)

This painting is typical of Prendergast's subject matter. He enjoyed painting idyllic scenes of beaches, parks, festivals, and landscapes filled with people enjoying their leisure time.

Prendergast was a member of The Eight, a group of painters who specialized in portraying everyday subjects. He participated in the group's only painting exhibition, which was held in New York City in 1908.

Greatly influenced by the French Post-Impressionists, Prendergast had a unique style of placing pure, bright colors side by side using broad brushstrokes.

This painting of Central Park in New York City looks like a decorative collage or mosaic of small pieces that when seen from a distance, combine to create a full landscape scene.

Keep Score: 11 Changes ☐ ☐ ☐ ☐ ☐ ☐ ☐ ☐ ☐ ☐ ☐

Frederic Remington
A Cavalryman's Breakfast on the Plains (c. 1892)

Filmmaker John Ford's epic western *She Wore a Yellow Ribbon* (1949) was directly inspired by Remington's work. He accurately recreated the composition of this painting for one scene in the movie and in interviews admitted that during filming he "tried to have the cameras photograph it as Remington would have sketched and painted it."

While attending Yale, Remington drew journalistic cartoons for the university's paper.

Remington produced over 3,000 drawings and paintings in his short lifetime (he died at the age of 48).

In addition to paintings, Remington enjoyed creating three-dimensional works of art. He completed 22 bronze sculptures of cowboys and other western scenes.

The artist left college in order to travel across the U.S. on horseback. During the journey, he worked as a cowboy and prospected for gold, all the while filling a diary with observations and collecting artifacts that he would later use in his paintings.

Keep Score: **10 Changes** ☐ ☐ ☐ ☐ ☐ ☐ ☐ ☐ ☐ ☐

Pierre-Auguste Renoir
The Umbrellas (1881-86)

Renoir painted this picture in two separate stages, beginning in 1881 and returning to it in the fall of 1885. The right-hand side of the canvas exhibits the softer brushstrokes and brighter colors of the artist's Impressionist style while the figures on the left, painted four years later, are more muted in color.

The fashions in this rainy day scene are also telltale signs of the change in time periods. The mother and children on the right are wearing elegant outfits at the height of 1881 fashion while the shop girl on the left wears a more tailored 1885 look.

Renoir was part of the Impressionist group of painters. He often painted outdoors to show the effects of light as realistically as possible.

Renoir was inspired to become an artist after a visit to the Louvre in Paris when he was about nine years old. Before he died, he was able to visit the museum and see his own paintings hanging there!

During the last 20 years of his life, Renoir was so crippled with arthritis that he found it difficult to paint. By strapping a brush to his hand, he was able to continue doing what he loved.

Around the time Renoir completed this painting, he began to veer away from Impressionism, drawing inspiration from the works of Ingres and a more classical style of art.

Keep Score:
10 Changes

☐ ☐ ☐ ☐ ☐
☐ ☐ ☐ ☐ ☐

Henri Rousseau
Flowers in a Vase (1909)

Rousseau did not begin to paint until he was almost 40 years old. He was an untrained, completely self-taught artist.

He is best known for his exotic jungle scenes, despite the fact that he had never left France or seen a jungle. Visits to the zoos and botanical gardens in Paris provided the inspiration for his imaginative art.

Rousseau held a job with the Paris Customs Office when he took up painting as a hobby. He retired from his job early, at age 49, so that he could devote his time entirely to art.

Rousseau's portraits, still lifes, and junglescapes are examples of a manner of painting known as "naïve," a term for an untrained artist that refers to his simple, childlike vision of the world.

Rousseau once said, "Nothing makes me happier than to contemplate nature and to paint it. Would you believe that when I go out in the country and see all that sun, all that greenery, and all those flowers, I sometimes say to myself, All that belongs to me, it does!"

Keep Score:

9 Changes

☐ ☐ ☐ ☐ ☐
☐ ☐ ☐ ☐

John Singer Sargent
Paul Helleu Sketching with His Wife (1889)

Also known as *An Out-of-Doors Study*, this impressionistic style painting features Sargent's close friend, Paul César Helleu and his wife Alice Guerin.

Although Sargent likely began this painting out-of-doors, he probably finished it in his studio. The discovery of a photograph very similar to this painting suggests that the artist occasionally used photography to help him with composition.

Sargent was also an accomplished pianist whose musical ability was nearly equal to his artistic talent. Music played a major part in his life and he used it to both inspire and calm him while painting portraits.

Known for his glamorous portraits of British and American high society at the turn of the century, Sargent's long list of rich and famous clients helped to make him the leading portrait painter of his generation.

Sargent completed over 500 portraits and 1,000 landscapes in his lifetime.

Keep Score: 9 Changes ☐ ☐ ☐ ☐ ☐ ☐ ☐ ☐ ☐

Georges Seurat
The Circus (1890-91)

The Circus was the third panel in a series by Seurat on the popular attraction of modern city life and its late-night entertainment offerings. The first two were titled *Parade* and *Cancan*.

This painting was Seurat's great unfinished work. Unfortunately, he died while still working on it at the age of 31.

Seurat invented a technique called Pointillism, or Divisionism, which uses small points or dots of contrasting colors to create brilliant hues that blend together through the eyes of the viewer. *The Circus* is regarded as one of the most impressive works using this technique.

Seurat completed seven very large paintings and about 500 smaller ones during his brief lifetime.

Seurat drew many different versions of his paintings, sometimes completing as many as thirty sketches to prepare for the final work. His painstaking method is often contrasted with the spontaneity of the Impressionists.

Keep Score:
12 Changes

☐ ☐ ☐ ☐ ☐
☐ ☐ ☐ ☐ ☐
☐ ☐

Charles Sheeler
Skyscrapers (1922)

Charles Sheeler is recognized as one of the founders of American modernism as well as one of the master photographers of the twentieth century.

In *Skyscrapers*, Sheeler emphasized the sheer magnificence of the cityscape.

Considered a master of "precisionism," a crisp, geometric art style, Sheeler spent most of his time painting images of machinery and structures commonly found in American industry.

The precisionist technique imitated the camera's perspective of the visual world.

Sheeler collaborated with photographer Paul Strand on *Manhatta* (1921), a fascinating short film of New York City that is regarded as a landmark in the history of American cinema. The artist would later focus on similar city motifs in his photography, painting, and graphic art.

Sheeler enjoyed portraying the formal geometry of American architecture of the early twentieth century in his works.

Keep Score:

13 Changes

☐ ☐ ☐ ☐ ☐
☐ ☐ ☐ ☐ ☐
☐ ☐ ☐

Diner

Johannes Vermeer
The Milkmaid (c. 1658-60)

Along with Rembrandt and Frans Hals, Vermeer is now counted as one of the greatest Dutch artists of the Golden Age. However, a century ago his paintings were little known and often misattributed.

Vermeer was known as the painter of light, and he used visual tricks such as contrast to gain depth in his paintings by placing areas of very bright light right next to dark, shadowy areas. In this painting, the wall behind the milkmaid is bathed in light, but her skirt is so dark that it makes her appear three-dimensional.

His works usually have a window at the left of the picture, and this one even has a broken windowpane in the second row!

Vermeer painted about 40 pictures during his lifetime. Only 36 of them survive today.

X-ray and infrared photography revealed that Vermeer had initially included a basket for sewing or laundry on the floor beside the foot warmer. He painted over it in his final version, focusing the viewer's attention on the act of pouring out the milk.

Keep Score:

11 Changes

☐ ☐ ☐ ☐ ☐
☐ ☐ ☐ ☐ ☐
☐

Élisabeth Vigée-Le Brun
Self-Portrait in a Straw Hat (1782)

Vigée-Le Brun painted over 40 self-portraits during her long career. In this one, she depicted herself as an artist holding her palette and brushes.

Vigée-Le Brun was greatly inspired by the Flemish master Peter Paul Rubens. She was so impressed with his portrait of Susanna Fourment (originally titled *Le Chapeau de Paille*, meaning *The Straw Hat*) that in this self-portrait, she imitated both the pose and setting and tried to obtain the same effects with light and shadow.

The daughter of a Paris artist, Vigée-Le Brun began to show a talent for drawing as a child. She grew up to be one of the most successful and prolific portrait painters in history.

Vigée-Le Brun painted nearly 900 portraits, landscapes, and historical paintings in her lifetime.

Most of her patrons were wealthy aristocrats, but her most important patron was the Queen of France, Marie Antoinette. She painted over twenty portraits of the queen, including the most well-known, titled *Marie Antoinette Holding a Rose*.

Self-portraits allow artists to experiment with their own identity, and to focus on how other people see them. Portraits also provide a glimpse into the past, showing us what people looked like and how they dressed long ago.

Keep Score:
10 Changes

☐ ☐ ☐ ☐ ☐
☐ ☐ ☐ ☐ ☐

54

Pages 10–11 Paul Cézanne
The Cardplayers

- Painting Added (van Gogh's *The Sheep-Shearers*)
- Pipe Removed
- Scarf Color Changed
- Hat Band Added
- Toothbrush Added
- Cloak Color Changed
- Drawer Removed
- Gold Coins Added
- Wristwatch Added

Pages 12–13 William Merritt Chase
A Friendly Call

- Artwork Changed
- Wall Hanging Reversed
- Top Hat Added
- Newspaper Changed to Magazine
- Flower Color Changed
- Dog Added

- Dress Color Changed
- Picture Removed
- Man Added
- Tote Bag Added
- Pillow Tassel Removed

Pages 14–15 Jacques-Louis David
The Emperor Napoleon in His Study at the Tuileries

- Napoleon Bald
- Clock Time Changed
- Clock Key Removed
- Silver Medal Removed
- Button Added
- Book Added
- Design on Chair Knob Removed

- Emblem Added to Chair Arm
- Sword Removed
- Buckle Removed From Shoe
- Word "David" Changed to "Livid" on Scroll
- Candle Flame Removed
- Lamp Shade Color Changed

Pages 16–17 Edgar Degas
Portrait of Edmond Duranty

- Book Shelf Taller
- Apple Added
- Title Added to Book
- Beard Longer
- Binder Clip Added
- Daffodils Added

- Date Changed
- Quill Pen Added
- Book Color Changed
- Jug Added
- Right Hand Angle Changed
- Framed Picture Added

Pages 18–19 Thomas Eakins
Max Schmitt in a Single Scull

- Kite Added
- Cloud Removed
- Canoe Color Changed
- Train Added
- Plane Added

- Tree Changed
- Oars Lifted
- Ducks Added
- Rower's Reflection Removed
- Rower's Shirt Color Changed

Pages 20–21 Paul Gauguin
When Will You Marry?

- Tree Branch Changed to Pine Bough
- Sky Color Changed
- Snake Added
- Knothole on Tree Added
- Tree Added
- Plate of Fruit Added
- Rock Added
- Blouse Color Changed
- Flower in Hair Changed
- Woman's Head Turned
- Person Added

Pages 22–23 Vincent van Gogh
Starry Night

- Star Removed
- Moon Reversed
- Hot Air Balloon Added
- House on Hill Added
- Waterfall Added
- Rooftop Color Changed
- Church Spire Taller
- Bat Added
- Train Added

Pages 24–25 William Harnett
Music and Literature

- Color Panel on Book Changed
- Book Removed
- Poe's Name Added
- Candle Lengthened
- Handwritten Note Reversed
- Sheet Music Cover Color Changed
- Quill Reversed
- The Word INK Added
- Spider Added
- Bookmark Changed (center)
- Corner of Sheet Music Repaired
- Bookmark Removed (left)
- Crack in Flute Removed

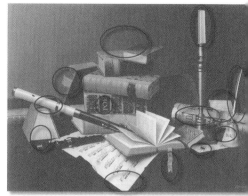

Pages 26–27 William Hogarth
The Graham Children

- Eyeglasses Added
- Cherry Added
- Dress Color Changed
- Girl's Head Turned
- Necklace Added
- Bird Added in Cage
- Birdcage Chain Changed
- Cat Removed
- Boy's Tie Color Changed
- Boy's Leggings Color Changed
- Handle on Floor Turned
- Candy Cane Added

Pages 28–29 Jean-Auguste-Dominique Ingres
Madame Moitessier

- Bracelet Changed to Watch
- Index Finger Removed
- Lipstick Added
- Hair Ribbon Color Changed
- Brooch Changed to Cameo
- Ring Color Changed
- Fan Changed to Book
- Pattern on Skirt Changed
- Book Added to Table

Pages 30–31 Édouard Manet
The Railroad

- Window Added at Top Left
- Jewel Added to Necklace
- Button Color Changed
- Puppy's Eye Open
- Bookmark Added
- Bar Removed From Fence
- Earring Removed
- Girl's Hair Color Changed
- Bird Added on Fence
- Grapes Color Changed

Pages 32–33 Claude Monet
Terrace at Sainte-Adresse

- Boat Removed
- Sailboat Reversed
- Hat Changed
- Smoke on Ship Reversed
- Bird Added
- Flag Changed
- Buoy Added
- Fence Changed
- Gopher Added
- Umbrella Color Changed
- Chair Removed
- Flower Removed

Pages 40–41 Pierre-Auguste Renoir
The Umbrellas

- Building Added
- Black Glove Added
- Umbrella Color Changed
- Girl's Face Changed
- Pant Leg Lengthened
- Bread Added to Basket
- Skirt Color Changed
- Necklace Added
- Beard Changed to Goatee
- Hat Changed to Baseball Cap

Pages 42–43 Henri Rousseau
Flowers in a Vase

- Tulip Color Changed
- Butterfly Added
- Flower Removed
- Stain Added to Table
- Ivy on Table Reversed
- Date Changed
- Snail Added
- Vase Changed
- Flower Added

Pages 44–45 John Singer Sargent
Paul Helleu Sketching with His Wife

- Duck Added
- Paddle Removed
- Easel Brace Changed to Fishing Rod
- Fish Added
- Paintbrush Changed to Crayon
- Feather Added to Hat
- Red Flower Added to Hat
- Picnic Basket Added
- JSS Added to Canoe

Pages 46–47   **Georges Seurat**
The Circus

- **Hat Removed From Man in Top Row**
- **Blouse Color Changed**
- **Girl Added**
- **Man Reversed**
- **Hat Removed**
- **Acrobat's Costume Color Changed**
- **Man Removed From Group at Right**
- **Flower on Lapel Color Changed**
- **Ringmaster's Shoe Points Up**
- **Red Nose Added to Clown**
- **Object Removed From Clown's Left Hand**
- **Horseback Rider's Head Reversed**

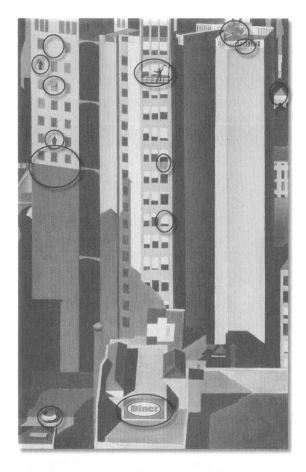

Pages 48–49   **Charles Sheeler**
Skyscrapers

- **Window Removed From Building at Left**
- **Woman Standing in Window Added**
- **Awning Added**
- **Curtains Added**
- **Shadow Line Changed**
- **Roof Fan Moved**
- **Window Washer Added**
- **Rug Hanging From Window Added**
- **Window Shade Lowered**
- **Billboard Sign Added**
- **Tree Added to Rooftop**
- **Penthouse Railing Changed**
- **Triangular Roof Color Changed**

Index